Hide!

words by Jill McDougall
illustrated by Leanne Argent

"Help!" said the mouse.

"The cat is after me."

"Hide in here," said a rabbit.

"Here she comes!"
said the mouse.

"Hide in here," said a bird.

"Here she comes!" said the mouse.

"Hide in here," said a fox.

"Here she comes!"
said the mouse.

"Hide in here," said a bear.

"Here she comes!"
said the mouse.

"Oh, no!" said the mouse.

"Here she is!"

"Help!" said the cat.

"The dog is after me."

"Don't hide in here," said the mouse.